Shards

Darius Rudominer

Presentation by *BookLeaf Publishing*

Web: www.bookleafpub.com

E-mail: info@bookleafpub.com

ISBN: 9789357444781

First edition 2022

DEDICATION

This book is dedicated to Sanjita and Crow, who carried me through this process with their wonderful words of encouragement, vicious slander, and in some cases edits on my own words that far outclassed any poetry I could've strung together myself.

Entropy

I like things cold, and spread apart;
Nothing close or stretched too far.
No work to do or dissipate,
No energy in resting state.
But sometimes I must stir from rest
(At my other half's behest)
to bind, and squeeze,
and shape,
and build,
and
w
o
r
k
until
the space is filled.
I do not mind to pull and haul
(for life is precious, after all)
But once i've worked my last reserve,
with mass and energy conserved,
I'll return at last to cold and spread,
at rest in my entropic bed.

Shards (kal)

There is no love in violence,
but there is violence in love.
It is the nature of small things,
to break in such
beautiful
shards

A most wonderful box

The sharps bin holds the sharp things
Needles, blades and broken glass
safely shield your fingertips
from scraps that bite and slash

Put the sharp things in the sharps bin
Ensure your safety check will pass
Clean the tear stains from your workspace
and toss them in the trash

The sharps bin is for sharp things
like wreckage from your crash
Put them in your sharps bin
accumulate your stash

Keep your sharp things in the sharps bin
your words like blades and broken glass
Keep them from your fingertips
don't let them out to slash

it's sterile in the lab today
the screens all dark and grey
buried in the datasheets
your heart forgets to beat

Break your sharp things in the sharps bin
your apathy and your gaze
Hide them from your friends until
your days pass in a haze

Find your sharp things in the sharps bin
your attention and your wit
Remember who you could've been
and find yourself adrift

Pick out your sharp things from the sharps bin
not all is torn to shreds
Suture kindness back again
with needle and a thread

Removal (kall)

I woke that morning like I
always had, bits of you
stuck in me like
      shards

      they never

      stung

      until

      they were
removed

Dark Flow

Something in the sky is pulling everything
towards it
it's too far away now

too long ago

I hope it's not alone

I think maybe we are

Roiling

Scrambling
from windswept beach
    Up and up the wave you
            reach

              (you hurt me)
       Hold your breath
    and count to ten
   The roil brings you
down
again

            (i'm sorry)

Fight the wave,
   you won't be thrown
     Hand on hand
       with claws
         of foam

         (sorry's not enough)
      Grasp the surf
     with desperate grip
    Down again
   the wave
you slip

        (i've tried everything)
Roiling with jaws of white
   You only ever learned to fight

       (try something else)
   Only one way left to go
Dancing with the undertow

Coping

My troubles have followed me doggedly from
yesterday to
today breathing damply down my neck;
like a dog,
I followed its tail from this day to the next,
and
the next,
and the next,
chasing myself away
and then stretching, reaching,
panting,
coming at last to face it in the shadow of dusk.
It greets me with
a familiar,
caring,
smile.
"Welcome home."

Non-Fungible

I thought you always wanted me
replaceable.
I thought your hunger to erase me was
insatiable.
I guess I should have known;
had to be something you could own.

We made this place for duplicating
unrestrainedly.
Wasn't it good to scale production
unattainably?
But there was nowhere left to grow,
and you just couldn't let it go.

You killed the stores to make more and
replace them again.
Now you're reinventing property to
chase that trend.
You moved your circus to the Cloud,
and I really hope you're proud.

Your self-worth was too easily expungeable.
I guess you'd better make it non-fungible.

Trust Function

The human does not trust the robot.
(This is clear from its biometrics:
its breathing, its
distance)

The robot knows what to do
in the absence of trust.
It reduces its turning rate,
and abruptness of motion.

The human's trust function is
unknown,
but can be estimated from its behavior.

So the robot observes:

The human returns to a spot
every day, from which sobs spike the robot's
sensors
and echo like feedback.

Humans need food.
It has been several hours since it was last in the
cafeteria,
and the sobs
have increased in volume. Perhaps the robot
should bring food?
But no, that suggestion is rejected
with force.

Some time ago, a robot was built for violence.
This robot was built for care.
The distance is as invisible
as breathing.

The human finds a plate in their cabin
after the sobs like feedback
have spent their force.
A function can change
with respect
to time.

Humans are not unlike robots,
after all, they too carry the shape of their
construction
into the present.

Face reveal!

At one million followers,
I will show you my Face.
Surely it must be precious
if I kept it so scarce.

Entangled

You and I, we always oscillate **together**
waveforms propagate to other **things** forever
As energy increases, with **many** orientations,
You and I and We could **be** infinite combinations
And yet it seems **to** me our bond is special
And this **is** not despite our many levels
We are both **alive,**
With this **To be** our tether:

Recombination (kalll)

I built my recombinant

                    Self from disparate

sources, chimeric, half
remembered

                  my ligase did not take

to the vestigial fragments

                        of you

Depth-First Search

I
dove
deep
and
drank
the
darkness
downward
I
determined
would
deliver
and
deliver
it
did
but
damn,   sometimes I think it was a scam

Missing

my trash is empty
I don't remember emptying it
but I suppose it must have been me
this is supposed to make me feel
                    lighter
the past always
was too

heavy

(A proof of consistency)

Let there exist an X
(both bounded and closed)
And let V be the set of sets
(and all things they enclose)

But if for all X there exists a Y
Such that X is in Y, then why
is there no set
that maps 1-to-1 with X?

One would expect uncountable sets
to hold infinite variation
And yet our fixed-point set here, X
is invariant to transformation

But X has never mapped bijectively
This pattern is quite persistent
Therefore it is consistent

(A proof of completeness)

Suppose there is a function
(a reasonable supposition)

Which is of course a bijection
(trivial to prove)

Then this function should provide
sufficient points to map
to everyone
(everything)
(of course)

It is trivial to prove
that this function
should go both ways
(don't you follow
my logic?)

It would be unjust to compete
of course it is
complete

(A proof by contradiction)

I used to think there was a hole in the world.
I thought we made our castles out of
sand until the surf washed away the
       contradictions
          at their
              foundation.

I won't complete the world, but maybe you
complete me.
Maybe I can be your
consistency.
Maybe
we can build our
           castles in the surf,
               laughing as we
   fall.

Gravitational

We pull each other
In greater or smaller ways
Across the world

Electromagnetic

These links between us
Some span merely a second
And some for lifetimes

Weak

Everyone makes bonds
Some decay explosively
It's okay to leave

Strong

We loathe loneliness
Against external pressure
Stable together